THE STUPEFYING

FROM THE AUTHOR OF

From the Author Of (2000)

Nonsense (2003)

Back with the Human Condition (2016)

Dandy Bogan: Selected Poems (2018)

Moral Sloth (2019)

THE STUPEFYING

NICK ASCROFT

**TE HERENGA WAKA
UNIVERSITY PRESS**

Te Herenga Waka University Press
Victoria University of Wellington
PO Box 600 Wellington
teherengawakapress.co.nz

A catalogue record is available at the National Library of New Zealand

ISBN 9781776920570

Printed in Singapore by Markono Print Media Pte Ltd

The first time I read the dictionary I thought it was a poem about everything.

—*Steven Wright*

Contents

// AFTER //

You Will Find Me Much Changed

After my brain injury I felt myself at a kink with the world.

After my brain injury I was no longer in tune with the sensibilities of the age.

After my brain injury I said things like, 'Fiction is over. Tell us the truth.'

After my brain injury I no longer found wonder in the universe.

After my brain injury I shrugged at butterflies, rainbows, the aurora australis, poison dart frogs, the apparent truth that the golden ratio presented the pressures upward and downward of the prices of stocks.

After my brain injury I obsessed over minutiae, such as the correct pronunciation of words, such as 'minutiae'.

After my brain injury I confused the bilabial nasal /m/ and the alveolar fricative sibilant /s/.

After my brain injury I walked with a lisp.

After my brain injury few could tell when I was joking or laughed at my jokes when they could.

After my brain injury I separated from my wife, arranging joint custody, which we did not call custody, and an agreeable division of assets, which we had some other mealy-mouthed term for also.

After my brain injury I found faces difficult to recognise, which had been the case before my brain injury.

After my brain injury I found the arts self-aggrandising, deceitful, flavourless, which ditto.

After my brain injury I was much unchanged.

After my brain injury, my short-term memory function declined, or continued to decline, but at a faster rate, or at the same rate if viewed against a logarithmic y-axis.

After my brain injury I was completely unchanged is another way to phrase it.

After my brain injury it was discovered I had fabricated the brain injury for attention. Some were unsurprised, which saddened me. Some thought the whole thing had been performance art, which disgusted me.

After the onset of my early onset dementia, I was wonderfully unawares, the onset being insidious.

After my diagnosis of early onset dementia nobody believed me because of the whole brain injury fabrication.

After I lost all neurological integrity, panting, gibbering, spasming, muttering and becoming a great burden to those around me, I found no solace in music.

After my death I was in a foul mood, and barked my opinion to anyone who would listen that opera was long-winded and unpleasant.

After I no longer existed and thousands of years had passed and no one remembered me and no record remained of anything I had ever been involved with and it made no sense for me to be a subject to which a predicate in the present tense was attributed, I whistled that tolerable bit of *Madama Butterfly* and considered whether I should add a caveat, in regards of my earlier attitude on opera, but who could I tell other than you, also non-existent at that point, and of course I no longer existed either, so I may as well have been telling you it before we were both born, if you follow, and nor had I existed when I expressed the first opinion, so it was best just to accept there was no going forward with the whole enterprise.

House, Kid, ~~Dog~~ Divorce

(for Kate at thirty-eight)

Things to file under H, K and D, respectively, shrug one's
hunchback and roll on to the next defeat. Or the next

success, or minor success, or catastrophe framed at a
skew and a squint so as to be overlain with a success

narrative. Like when I tumbled off the bike at speed onto
my elbow, and a concerned passerby asked if I was
okay, thereby activating the needless-positivity

mechanism. I am overjoyed. I am a picture of bright
health. Ignore the blood. There is a song I want to sing you
about the rapture of the road. You have a beautiful

smile, and if I was not a coward I would use this rare
social opportunity as a screwball meet cute, asking you

to coffee. You might feel at first obliged, then repelled,
then, strange chemistries of the air eddying, drawn in.

The passerby persisted, my sunshine unconvincing. I am
okay, I said. The years pass and I am okay. The blows
come. From the left – WHAM – the right – SMACK – from

below into the groinal area. Some I invent. Some I
overindulge. Some I blank. I'm okay. I am okay. You

could knock back antidepressants, but who would you
become? For all the weight gain, nausea, dry mouth and

constipation you might as well be pregnant again. Your
doctor says you should. Your father says you would be
crazy not to. Your sister is sceptical of Western

medicine's bombast, but thinks you should take the pills.
Even I, from whom you only want unwavering support,
will soon enough mutter something small and traitorous.

Everybody in New Zealand is today older than they have
ever been, and no one is thrilled about it. But we kick

away from such sourpuss energy, surrounding ourselves
with the vivid and magnificent. The inspirational. The

sharp-witted and truthful. The effortlessly diplomatic.
The handy with power tools. Or you do. While I slump into
the wings, making a big show of wishing you well.

Heroic. Intermittently tragic. Not at all the crossed-out
dog in the title that nobody has suggested I was. And the
curtain call brings me back onstage anyway to be pelted

with flowers and fruit. I applaud us. You keep the house,
or sell it. We love the blasted kid. And the seventeen

years together are untouchable in their glory and peril.
And for the next? Let 2038 tell its own well-earned epic.

Poem for Derek

I understand that to have a poem dedicated to you
is a horrifying burden.

No one wants it, Derek.
I am witnessing your face muscles warp
of their own accord as I announce
to whom it goes out.
Springs in a mattress recoiling under psychic bulk.

How are you required to react?
I am giving you a printout.

What are you supposed to do with it?
Frame it on a wall in your house, so that everyone
sauntering past stops and says, huh,
a poem? For you, is it?
Yes.

But which wall? The bedroom wall would be creepy.
A corridor, too obvious. The kitchen, unavoidable.

The bathroom, cretinous.
The funny little man-cave in the basement
you had intended to spend more time in
then never managed to convince anyone
to come down with you and it's somehow boring

to be anywhere on your own for too long, Derek?
Yes.

Your name isn't Derek of course.
No one is called Derek, the word-aura

bringing to mind a smell of damp and parsnips.
Unless spelled D-E-R-R-I-C-K
and it comes with a story of a small arms manufacturer

and an Irish valley innkeeper.
I can't be so cruel as to use your real name

and have the thing hung on you for the remainder,
everyone saying, it's so-and-so
that had the poem written for them.
You are not a wall in your own man-cave
and deserve better than that.

Shakespeare kept shtum
so as not to embarrass thingbob.

Lucretia Nairn had that Keats number changed
to 'a Grecian Urn'. She had baulked:
'unravish'd bride of quietness'? Do me a favour!
Why does anyone have a poem aimed at them
is the question.

Answer: to get into their pants.
As if a poem wouldn't have

the absolute opposite effect.
And what sort of pants might a poem provide access
into? Not any pants you should
wish to find yourself in, Derek.
Only the most despicable pants, which,

once inside, one would howl and attempt exit from
at all costs and rapidly.

Luminous and Shimmering Writing

No poem shimmers. No writing is luminous.
It's black text on an off-white background.
If you see any shimmering or luminosity,

you have a migraine.
A woman in a beret at the front of the bus

turns around and pulls in one cheek.
She suggests that might be over-literal.
They mean luminous in an abstract sense

and, you know, figurative shimmering.
How so though?

Luminous in clarity? Not a bit.
Shimmering in vagueness, shimmering
in unconscious connectivity

or dreamscape? Could be, says beret.
The gut says, you know what I think?

You want to know what I think though?
We brace ourselves.
The gut lends itself to obsolete opinions.

We nod for it to continue.
What I think we've got is sugarwork.

Luminous means good. Shimmering just
means good. It's a bit of prettying up and all
you can taste is the cloying and marzipan.

Sarcasm Is the Lowest Form of Whist

Sarcasm is . . .
the lowest form of limbo.
the tallest monkey puzzle tree in Mid-Canterbury.
the lowest note on the piano, and sounds like *murrr*, almost unmusical.

Sarcasm is . . .
an archaism of an orgasm.
the least impotent of all rage.
less cutting than cutty sarcasm, which is a meaningless play on whirs.

(Cutty means short and sark means shirt.
So in 'Tam o' Shanter' by Robert Burns when the witches
cast off their rags to reel to the devil's bagpipes,
they are left wearing only nightie-like underthings.)

Sarcasm is . . .
the lowest incantation of witchery.
the bottommost and blackest depth of wit, which is a compliment,
the lowest form of compliment.

Niki's Handbrake in Tokorozawa, 2004

'Let's go,' she'd said, her finger indicating
straight into the maze of streets, all signs
in Japanese, and apps weren't syndicating
maps back then – no phones – no beers nor wines
as yet to fire our blood, all vindicating
my position, having no designs
on getting lost here. I'd squeaked: 'What?'
And doubled down with: 'Absolutely not.'

That's Niki, unencumbered by a proper
dread of things. And me, a yellow streak
of cowardliest custard – each a stopper
on the other's excess. Well, she let me speak,
and I encouraged caution from the cropper
crouched in wait. And that was our mystique:
the bold – her – and me – frettable. There tends
to be a balance to the world with friends.

We ventured out eventually, once Blair,
our host and guide and speaker of the lingo,
cycled home. He had two bikes, one fair
and new, I complimented it, and bingo,
it was mine, with Niki riding there
on Yoshie's. Past ramen joints, pachinko
halls and smoke we slid, the bar too, smoky.
Afterwards we'd go to karaoke.

But first we drank, she smoked, I ate, but *what*?
No meat-free food I ordered managed to
be free of meat – still pious, and a spot
anaemic, then – some gristle bandaged to

tempura made for dinner. I was not
delighted. Blair had Niki sandwiched to
an aisle, meanwhile, to draw the lady in.
She rolled her eyes, and a Canadian

came to her aid. I mean he flirted too, this guy,
clean cut in specs, inhaling Ventolin –
but while I'd seen a few give it a try –
none yet had been so much a gentleman.
Self-designated secretary was I
of her affairs (op. cit.), and pencilled him
a tick. Yes I was ever dutiful,
appraising those who found her beautiful

and bold, not that I had the acumen
to be of any use. But it was nice
to influence, and as a pack of them
were always queuing up, my free advice
just must have been – well in a vacuum – an
advantage. Some? My mouth was full of rice
this time, but up stepped the Canuck,
reminding Blair he was a dodgy fuck,

who still had Yoshie at home. I guess
he had a point. But I prefer economy
in morals, balance. Niki could express
herself: allow her the autonomy,
I thought. No undue need to overdress
my role, or too highly honour me.
I wasn't Niki's chaperone, nor Blair's,
and thank their lucky stars I wasn't theirs.

No, mine. I meant vice versa. As the booze
is starting to confuse me, I should wing
the story on. We left the bar, and shoes
to pedals headed for a moonlight sing.
The type of song is always hard to choose.
I went for some glam (cancelled) nineties thing.
(My nasal voice is yet to win a trophy.)
She picked a minor hit by Jon Bon Jovi.

The verse was tricky though – she knew the chorus –
but . . . When Niki's voice came through the mic
it wasn't bold, just tentative and porous.
Sake and the beers had loosed the dyke
that held my inhibition: I was raucous
in the back-up. Howling lionlike,
I drowned her out, quite chivalrous in truth,
though just the three of us were in the booth.

We cycled homeward. Boldness overcame
my wheels. I glimpsed the red but scanned the road
ahead and saw no traffic. My bike's frame
was light. It loved the speed, and madly mowed
the distance through the dark, my gills aflame.
But as I made the junction, headlights glowed
just to my right. In my embroidered state
I clenched both brakes too hard, but not too late.

Flung off I thudded helmetless against
the road. My skull by luck is thick. By morning
sure, I had a headache, which ring-fenced
a grim hangover, and a cold was warming
up to boot. The worst thing as I woke I sensed
had been the thumbs. The force that sent me soaring

forward wrenched the hand brakes from my grip.
No judgement, Niki helped me with my zip

and hair tie – huge and blue and functionless,
my thumbs – a balance as I say that held
our friendship, neither of us gumptionless
or timid at all times. Some were compelled
to think I also found her scrumptious. This
was not the thing at all. We simply gelled.
Ah, never analyse what is inscrutable.
We were the bold and the refutable.

Why I Changed My Surname

It's 1989 – imagine me
in shorts. The first line is a test, to check
you have the stomach for the pageantry.
If my unusual shape in shorts, and heck,
all gangly, glossy, mumped and badgerly
of face – think puberty's Toulouse Lautrec –
won't race you to the sink, and if the glare
of 1989 itself, the year

that culture died in lemon shoulder pads,
can fail to summon up a migraine, well,
I shake your hands. I do. It really adds
a grit to your appeal. I can tell
that you're all better cunts than I, comrades.
Now buttered up, read on, I'm here to sell
a tale so harrowing in woe you'll quake.
I'm cycling back from French, the class I take

not at Waitaki Boys', but Girls', the lone
and solitary boy, and only boy
arrayed in shorts. I'm shy, and keep the cone
my gaze projects aimed low. They don't annoy
me, girls – my sisters say, or Christians blown
across the south, from Gore to Kaiapoi.
For co-ed summer camps I'm good to go.
I have no friends in French class though.

Felicity is kind at least, her name
itself a squeal of eightiesesque pizazz –
the sheen and glitz – more, though, provincial shame.
She deigns to talk to me. It's lucky as

there's only her among us who can tame
the tongue. She has the chops. And since she has,
to pair with her for orals is a win.
(A word I find no innuendo in,

blessed as I am with innocence.) Forget
those girls, however, and the pain of waiting
at the door as others dawdle past and let
out gasps and point – a boy! – I'm contemplating
all things low like shoes and concrete (*set
these shoes with concrete, drop me in a strait*) and
gritting teeth until Monsieur can like
a-fucking-rrive. I've shot off on my bike,

returning to a boys' high calculus
classroom, and wearing, as I say, my shorts.
A wasp, whose keg is far from powderless,
flies up, so self-absorbed in waspish thoughts,
to where my pedalling has allowed her this
route in. My shorts close up, and she retorts.
I yelp and thrash and make a lot of rumpus.
My first thought is I've pocketed a compass

by mistake, when reaching for a pen.
The barb goes in and out and in, then bzzz
I see the bastard wasp fly out again.
She pauses at my bell and glares because
I fail to act contrite. The stings' cayenne
has caused my hip to bubble up and fizz,
where histamines flood an anomaly.
It sears. No wasp believes in comedy.

The agonies these allergies provoke
are not the subject of the woe that I
am here to wail about. A wasp may poke
with its envenomating end one's thigh
and, sure, the memory may arouse baroque
responses from the mind in future. (My
long arms aloft, years later I am streaking
round the garden of a pub and shrieking

as a wasp manoeuvres right and left,
in hot pursuit, or does so in my head.
My friends, while supping at their beers, bereft
of pity, tut.) But other pains are said
to lead to deeper warpings of the weft
that shapes the fabric of the self, and dread
of self, as here. The taunts of others' loathing
are internalised and worn as clothing.

Returning to my school for maths, I'm met
by a parade of boys, as every day, who prate
their mantra at me on the walkways: get
a haircut, get a fuckin' haircut, mate.
I laugh or roll my eyes, I'm no courgette,
but if they're huge and tottering with hate,
I'll dash and cut the corner of the quad.
I think they're fools and feel like a god.

That is, I have a staunch belief this bilge should
never get to me, they're dicks, and I'm
correct to grow my mop and feel a pilchard
only during this protracted time
of hair-as-eiderdown because this quilt should
rise just to a certain height then climb

back down, dragged into velvet twists of chain,
like on my wall, thrash metal's Dave Mustaine.

I err. Not only is it wearisome
to be abused and told by every kid
from sweaty pipsqueak through the fairydom
of bronze-beige cricketers that this, the squid
atop my head, is hateful, and so drearisome
the jeer as I, like an elaterid,
ascend the stair to the assembly dais
for the reading (of which they'll repay us

with the reading prize again, my bellow
so melodic) – but it also scratches
in. For it to be the norm one's fellow
pupils find one hideous dispatches
knowledge, which the liminal marshmallow
of the self absorbs and can't detach, is
interchangeable with fact: you're frightful.
Your physiognomy is undelightful.

I get the other classic line while ducking
back to sit, some disembodied random
from behind says I look like a fucking
girl (which I should chalk to gay abandon),
then the usual squall of turkey clucking.
This 'Nick-Brook-Nick-Brook-Nick-Brook' is fandom,
says the rector's deputy, who hauls
me to his office – deluded utter balls –

and that he fears I'll devastate prizegiving
with my rabble-rousing hair, thus must
he clip my wings, or curls, these outsize living

epithets of insurrection, just
to flatten any hope, or likewise sieving
of the lay of land for nuggets of mistrust
for institutions by the weak or dim.
He sends me home to give my hair a trim.

I bring the scissors close but only flail
at the front and, weeping, make a fringe.
The rest I wrench into a ponytail.
I look a tit, but tidy, and the cringe
is brief, one chop's not made a phoney pale
shadow of myself, it won't impinge
upon my will to grow my locks, and yet
I shuffle back to school reduced, upset.

This wasn't 1989. I run
kaleidoscopes of memory together.
1990, 1991:
the shorts, the gobbling, girls, French, wasps, the heather
of my hair? Who cares. Like everyone
I suffered through my teens. But whether
I was stung enough to cause the mess
I make of life? It's possible I guess.

Cross-Eyed Martyr

Get off the cross: we need the wood pulp for junk mail.

Get off the cross. You're in my selfie, babes.

Get off the cross, Raymond!

Get off the cross. Take a deep breath. I've poured you a nice glass of water. Make sure to hydrate sufficiently, then get back on the cross.

Get off the cross. Get off the grass. Get off the crack pipe. Get off the grid. Get off my foot.

Get off the cross. That cross anyway. It's a UNESCO heritage cross. You're more a plywood cross guy.

Get off the cross! It's a crime scene and you're just bleeding all over it.

Get off the cross at Paddington and change to the Bakerloo line. This train terminates at self-immolation.

Get off the cross. It's filthy, and that's a brand-new shirt.

Off the cross, get you, padawan. Wood we need, yes.

Get off the cross, that's meant for the top of my bun. I'll see myself out.

Get off the cross: we need the nails. Well, two of them. You'll have to balance.

Get off the inflatable cross. Conceptual art is best left in the madcap early 2000s.

Fenton! *Fenton!*

Get off the cross: we are bulldozing the area for a townhouse development.

Get off the cross, Baby Jesus!

('Why didn't I think of that?' says the Babe, and the nails tug themselves out of the wood, slipping through wrists and metatarsals and falling to earth like snowflakes, while the little dude shoots off into the sky.)

Get off the upside-down cross, you daft Satanist.

('I'm not a Satanist,' says St Peter, crucified feet-to-the-sky – apocryphally, surely – so as not to imitate his Lord, but kind of in a show of one-upmanship too, and the Romans had said, 'Whatever you like St Pete. Prisoner's choice.')

Get off both of those crosses. Sorry no, I'm just very high.

Great-Grandad Rants over Current Affairs

News! Where is it if not in newspaper, black type a printer set?
  The internet.
If there's a custard emergency or yoghurt issue,
some armed blasted insurgency in Mogadishu,
or a celebrity opened their beak and deigned to speak to pondslime,
where is it? Online.
And sport? To what wireless does one sear one's ears to hear the footfall
of jelly-legged idiots prancing after a football?
Or if some goon lobs a Frisbee, or a cherub swats a golf tee, SLAP?
Where do you find that crap?
  That app.
In my day was the news ever fake?
  No! Every dawn the front page said SHEEP TRAPPED IN LAKE
  or GIRL DRESSED AS MERMAID
  or THE WEATHER'S A BIT HOT
  or TOWN ERECTS STATUE OF GIGANTIC APRICOT.
But now if there's no news, then what?
  Before they flip the channel on
  get a panel on.
What if no one's listening? The news must be shrieked!
What if journalism's dead? The news must be leaked!
They have every minute of the year to fill,
and with what? Codswallop, hogwash, humbug and swill.
What is news anyway? Young ladies and lads, comrades,
  Look up from your doodads and iPads.
What is it, news? Whatever sells ads.

Silver Vixen

You can't write sexy poems
if you are a grandmother, but
pshaw says I to such yokelism,
oppressive custom
and snippiness.
I will say what I want and writhe
on the floor in
ecstasy as I do so.
Another zombie and I once leapt

on the waterbed and
did jazzercize!
Our limbs were slippery
as horse limbs
after a boxed quinella
if you follow my racing-related
innuendo.
Tongues licked where angels
feared to boogaloo. Thighs

applauded. I wriggled
my clavicles and scapulae, all
fizzy
and delighted that
the inner animal acted
as the generations
had impelled it. I didn't let it
finish, but
held it shivering at the verge . . .

Fifty Poems for Kim

1972, first birthday
No real linguistic competence at this age, and a whistly memory, so I won't bother.

1973
Ditto, or enough ditto to just get away with it.

1974
Can't get a word in edgeways. Jesus.

1975
One rhyme then I duck off to buy cereal: aubergine/go-between.

1976
Never shake a five-year-old. Never. Unless it's choking on a rissole.

1977
Here's Kim, knee-high, snipping round the paddocks on all fours barking.

1978
Aristotle said give me the girl, shrugging at your blathering at seven, and I will terrify you with the woman.

1979
Disco wigs in Woolworths.

1980
Scooby Doo, Scooby Dee, Scooby Dah-ha-ha-ha-ha. Puberty.

1981
Your mother wrecks another rather wobbly Christmas.
Your father decks your brother at your property's isthmus.

1982
But Doreen is a whizz at the electric frypan.

1983
Here's Kim, a snarler of pipes.

1984
Kim again, a parlour of snipes.

1985
Bruno Lawrence in a frock. The planet Saturn hovering at the sea's
horizon.

1986
Europium is a toxic heavy metal created in a neutron star merger.
Europe's 'The Final Countdown' is similar but the exact opposite.

1987
Some biker rogers Kim in her school kilt.

1988
The was a young girl from Orawia
With a heart hard and deep as Lake Hāwea, etc.

1998
[Poem removed by pervert for disgusting purposes.]

1990
Travelling from town to town, having adventures, solving crimes,

kicking arse and taking photographs. Cue funk-metal credits theme tune.

1991
Ah, the UTIs of youth. Stick those in your piss-hole.
Never bed a drummer. Unless he's choking on a rissole.

1992
There is no predicament or entanglement one can't take a breath, look into the eyes of, and honourably flee from.

1993
Here's Kim, seeing dead people in a Queenstown scullery. Quit chat. Unfazed.

1994
Dunedin! Crashed while taking crashed while taking Dunedin! Crashed while off taking crashed please. Crashed! While stop please Dunedin! Crashed while taking off Gaylene.

1995
I went down to the crossroads: Albany and Queen.

1996
Hot knives to the element!

1997–99
[Poems removed by mawkish-bullpucky police.]

2000
Visit old boss sent to Rolleston Prison for NOTHING, just trying to fly in ephemeral quantities of cocaine to sell.

2001
Hot spoon to the earlobe!

2002
The golden hills of Otago
pickled in tussock and freckled with sheep turds
doze into gorges.

2003
Here's Kim the trainee social worker goggling at the awfulness.

2004
The rat dog is loosed downstairs and sidewinds into their bedroom.
Kim squeaks. Andy groans a nooo.

2005
Kim again, cooing like a mogwai
the sad song
of parting and furballs.

2006
Here's Andy, dressed as a pangolin,
long-tonguing termites off her eyeballs.

2007
Roses are red and sidelocks Hasidic.
Milk is alkaline, cheese acidic.

2008
Here's Kim in Oxford, England, not Oxford, North Canterbury,
eyes twinkling sweet evil like limoncello.

2009–2011
[Removed. Are these even poems? I mean that's probably a compliment. But I cull them for pedantry.]

2012
How long is this fucking life?

2013
Long enough to have thankfully avoided children. Her cervix seals over like a neglected nose-ring hole. Here's Kim perhaps with the lucky stars never to be forced to watch *Frozen*.

2014
The world flirts with the notion of karma, but there's too much to keep track of. *Did I already get that guy back for . . . ? Whoa what's this bitch doing??*

2015
I'm-not-nostalgic-you're-nostalgic, thumbing through old photo albums: Gretel resplendent, Niki teetering, Nick Cameron cross-eyed.

2016
Cheese is an acid, milk's a base.
Penises (flaccid) splatter your face.

2017
Here's Duncan, hammering on the other side of the frosted glass with his fists while Kim nods.

2018
Kim with a fleet of one car
ushers Americans
around their own monologues.

2019
The most precious of jagged jewels
is the kidney stone
blasted by extracorporeal shock wave lithotripsy.

2020
Here's Kim and Andy's pimped and primped new pad, in a
post-lockdown upgrade.

2021
Life is a cunt,
then you laugh a slightly too high-pitched HA,
then you die.

1988

1988 welcomes you. The Proclaimers are unembarrassed by their Christianity, singing that while 'the Chief puts sunshine on Leith' they will continue to be appreciative. And if not? Unknown. R.E.M. have a wah-wah guitar that questions why you have the place you stand in. Bobby McFerrin has no worries at all, and lightly admonishes you that your frown is depressing passersby. The solution is perplexing in its simplicity: be happy and, perhaps as a way there, don't worry. Roy Orbison suddenly croons that he is so tired of being lonely in the middle of a Traveling Wilburys song, and the others quickly segue into an upbeat chorus that might be about dreaming your way into a true connection but is more likely an attempt to dazzle some unfortunate into a root. Leonard Cohen is creepy for sure, but his rhyming 'Everybody's talking to their pockets' with 'chocolates' pleases our giddy inner nihilist, achieving what we feel guilty Bobby McFerrin didn't. The Close Lobsters have a guitar sound you can hug. The House of Love likewise, but are ultimately soppy in the song 'Destroy the Heart'. Not destroying the heart is what they advocate. Not destroying it, despite what you say, because in an eruption of hyperbole the fictitious romantic organ is assigned more necessity than air. Jangle welcomes you. The Dunedin Sound's greatest compilation *In Love with These Times* should welcome you, but its release is delayed a year. Power ballads welcome you. Hair metal welcomes you. Metallica twirl their mullets in AFFRONT. Yes they condition their tresses, but they are not hair metal. Instead in 'Eye of the Beholder' they buoy incels and anti-vaxxers with a vision of the mainstream's hypocrisy: freedom of choice, freedom of speech, freedom of parking, all are freedoms 'with *their* exception!' Bret Michaels of Poison has no such anachronistic and sententious pretensions. Instead he is a rose, whose thorns cut women, and he feels just terrible about it. But that's roses! What can you do? Axl Rose whistles. Ozzy Osbourne and Lita Ford have a *Remains of the Day* thing going, and are both threatening to murder themselves in 'Close My Eyes Forever'. It is high camp and wonderful. 'There she goes,' notice the La's. The Cure are more florid about it: 'itching, squealing, fevered' and the like. Jane's Addiction's eponymous Jane is fevered too but she's going to kick tomorrow. Or 'live and die this way,' as Tracy Chapman warbles in 'Fast Car'. Then it's the perfect past tense that kills you in the chorus: she *had* a feeling she belonged; she *had* a feeling she could be someone. Few seem to be adhering to Bobby McFerrin's happiness diktat. Morrissey bucks the trend. No he doesn't, but again the idea of your seaside town, which is of course Oamaru, begging for nuclear war is uplifting, the sweet fallout dropping onto your person like 'a strange dust'. Welcome to 1988. The Pet Shop Boys are here: look away. The Bangles are here: turn a grudging head. Sinéad O'Connor is unassailable and incandescent and yet to have her big hit. The year is a land of opportunity that thousands of us are sailing towards (to mangle the Pogues). A land, it must be conceded, that some of us will never see, or will quickly move on from.

Therefore We Commit This Body to the Ground

Dust to dust. Aluminium to aluminium.
Polypropylene plastic with a little 5 debossed
inside a triangular uroboros to something else
ideally, yes another type of thermoplastic,

but we don't have the facilities at the present time.
There was talk of those plastic-eating microbes,
visions of bacterial excreta
that had depolymerised the stuff

to only semi-toxic nitrides and acids,
but the microbes balked
at the crystalline structure of polypropylene,
preferring polyethylene terephthalate and its ilk.

Production will assault a giddy new high
of 100 million tonnes in 2022.
What do you want to store your shampoo in?
A tin can, like an animal?

Paper to paper. Recycled paper to ash.
Ashes to en dashes.
Human-to-human contagion.
Business-to-business marketing. Dust to thingbob.

Pishy-Caca, as My Doppelganger Ryan Gosling Says in *La La Land*

I've pissed on a piston, pissed in a pistol.
I've penned a puissant epistle to the unappeasable
legions of pissant Ephesians. I've pieced together
untethered letters,
sellotaped the tatters and sent most of them
back to their slack typesetters via post to them.
I've recouped couped-up grey geese in a coup de grace.
I've souped up uncoupled Gorbachevisms,
troubled uncomplicated dumplings
with visions of cuttlefish and octopus. I've socked
of course the lockjaws of doctors,
a subtle southpaw to the mouth, knuckles dusted
in cufflinks. I've clinked on Stuff links.

Couples Therapy

The couples therapist lived in Highbury, down
a sudden little valley. We parked the car
near the top and toe-heeled the slope,
making jokes,
the way the walking dead do.
Through the door there was some brickwork
and also wood panelling. Nothing is more
reassuring than brickwork and wood panelling.
I take it back; there was a 1970s laissez-faire
in the sunken lounge with a log burner near
the steps down in. A large glass ornament was
incongruous though, on a table
just distant of the three chairs.
I would look it at from time to time and frown.
The chairs were deep and soft, but it would
feel inappropriate to loll back into that softness
and really enjoy
what the chair seemed to delight in offering.
Mostly I perched

on the edge and held my fingers interlaced,
in a way I imagined my father would do when
looking attentive and priestly. Walking back
out to the car, we joked some more, but
in the car, safe
from the ears of the dark and leaf-sodden street,
we recapped a little, talked more.
Had the couples therapist taken my side too
much? I wasn't sure that she had, but another
analysis presented itself to me. Perched there
with my interlaced hands, not crying

or expressing anguish
and turmoil, I was the most polite.
I was thoughtful,
eager. You were trying to utter your truths, and
I was nodding, buoying up, validating,
commiserating, but,
also, trying
to get the couples therapist to take my side.

I Am a Lazy Art Critic Bot for Jon Cox's Canvases

(compiled from unhelpful Instagram messages)

i
The Bible meets Kafka in a whorehouse.

ii
Should be the new New Zealand flag.

iii
The record is off the groove for Cox. A gasket popped, he's plastering the wall with slag, melt and scrud.

iv
Nice specks. High spec. Spexy.

v
Scratch and sniff eggs and vegetables boiled colourless, Cox confronts the grunting appetites of the weary.

vi
Lots of cocks in that one.

vii
Needs more red. MORE REDDDDDD. No it's nice. Basic perhaps, but nothing wrong with hitting a birdie on a short par 3.

viii
Barbecue needs a clean.

ix
Barney the Dinosaur used to jizz LSD. Woe betide any fun-seeker lunching on that maelstrom.

Enhanced Interrogation

I'd only just remembered what Rick Astley
called his other hit: 'Together [*heave*]
Forever'. I'd intended to tell Ashleigh.
Then when sneaking into Kate's to thieve
some milk for Scrabble club that night, the song
was gurgling from her kitchen radio.
I wondered why I felt a hurt so strong
and so familiar. Shrugging – hey-de-ho,
that's living: agony – but then it struck
me. My old Casio! The track it squawked
on demo mode, all tinny clank and cluck.
And just now in an Uber, tomahawked,
again. It's haunting: 'never [*gah*] to part'?
What never? Yes. The torture is the art.

The Last Birthday Poem
for an Undefined Period

(on the occasion of her 39th, to Kate,
my friend and co-parent)

It's the last time I'll think of it
out loud, and won't give you

the poem itself on your birthday
because nostalgia and

the sour-sweet have their place,
which is not amidst a celebratory

mood, but I think of the hillside
in Hawke's Bay where I

choked up a little but said
my vows and you said yours

and for the time we meant them.
Everyone we were most

indebted to was there. Kushana,
Paula, your dad, family, and mine,

my father muttering to the end
of a gem I brushed the gist of,

Kim, Andy – not Niki – though
even there I felt bad about it.

I see all their eyes on us and
there's a twang of a string I can't

articulate, but could pick at.
I hear the worst of the phrases,

and in my high nasal voice:
for better or worse. I don't

strum at it. I feel the twang,
and to feel it, it helps me move

through it. I see the new rapport
ahead and embody it, my friend.

The Third and Most Stupefying Bike Spill

Not the one, nine or ten years old, where the little fingers
of the front forks, one moment pinching hold of the wheel
as they should, the next, squinched free: PING. And over and down

I sailed, the wheel christening the back of my head as it bounced.
Crying in the bathroom with Mum, not at the pain,
but the gore, a raspberry-red semicircle skinless below my thumb,

I saw it in her face, at last. What could she do, five years younger
than I am today? Only later did I appreciate that I had amputated
a wart, and I would never grow another. Until the jinx curse

just now. The bike blew around my paper-run at top speed in
every weather, which in Te Anau meant rain, with a variability
on slant. Each morning, before the van chugged in from Invercargill

with the papers, my sister and I would perform 'amazing stunts'.
We would double each other, the two of us on one bike
in ever more adventurous combinations. Her on the handlebars.

Me kneeling backwards on the carrier. She stood on her hands.
I balanced one-legged like the Karate Kid. Occasionally
an early-rising local or the delivery van driver would warn us

to be careful. We were not careful, but never crashed or toppled off.
Our bicycles were pieces of old junk – as made clear when
the wheel deserted me riding sensibly in a straight line – but we

were always on them and they felt extensions of our will.
I blame this on my third and most stupefying adult bike spill.
I was not so drunk when I was ten, but the sensation of control,

despite clownish swoops to the left and right, was the same.
When the front wheel hit the gutter and the bike slopped over,
it was like every crash, sudden, inevitable. Of course it was;

if crashes weren't sudden or inevitable there would be time to make
some compensatory twist. It slopped over and I came down hard
on the shoulder. The next day a chemist helped me tie a sling,

and the day after the doctor's eyes were like my mother's:
What to do with you? Take the sling off, she said. The joint needs
to move. My left arm still cringes like a lobster claw, creaking

around in a painful shell. But who can pity me? You can.

// DURING-SLASH-BEFORE //

Unhelpful Signage

Wanton endangerment inadvisable beyond this line

Restrict amplitudes to those that fail to perforate spongiform envelope of my patience

Marriage in progress

This door must remain closed: for ingress or egress only

Use eggshell path on tippy-toes to circumnavigate room's elephant

Shh, I'm watching this ad

If mental load exceeded, break glass with one hand, defibrillate with other and I still need your timesheets

Read the letters on the bottom line in order

N O A L P H A B E T I C A L O R D E R Y O U F A I L

They're Playing the 'You've Gone on Too Long' Music, but the Essential Struggle Is to Think Yourself More Important Than the Schedules of Plebeians

Jean-Paul Sartre said the essential struggle
was not to become a pastiche of yourself,
sleepwalking through the motions

of your day like an automaton – if automata
can sleepwalk – I'm paraphrasing –
squirting out your front door in a flap every
morning, chasing down the bus,
29 minutes on Twitter, mumble-shouting
ANGST
DRIVER
as you disembark, huffing up the stairs
and buzzing from meeting room to meeting
room like the fluorescent lighting the LED
lighting has replaced – I'm paraphrasing,
the guy wrote in French – sulking through
lunch, procrastinating through the twilight
sleepy time of 2 till 3, then a burst, then a
cup of tea, then a burst, then a fire-fight

over an email you missed from a higher-up
you must cringe before like a worm –
if automata can cringe like worms – and

science fiction isn't exactly convincing
on this point – then no time to wee before
hustling buswards and homewards,

sitting too close to a man that smells like sour
vase water, rain pulverising the bus's carapace,
wind scissoring your eyes as you –
ANGST
DRIVER –
lollop home all top-heavy like a popsicle
in your coat, kiss your spouse, your cat,
your child, who screams blue bedlam till
bedtime, then chirps, fends, parries, squawks,
finally succumbing to sleep's hammer,
and the day judders – the dishes wash
themselves as your hands schuck at the sink

with a pot scrubber – then grinds: the couch
has an impression you slouch neatly into
for half of a streamed episode while

stabbing at your phone, nodding while your
spouse speaks, then the dark of sleep calls,
you wee at last, undress in identical motions
of the day before, collapse, wake at 2
to bring the child through, the dark resumes,
wake at 5 when the cat decrees it with claws
and singing, lock him in the kitchen,
steal one half hour more from the shadows,
then the day repeats. Or to add the agency
that Jean-Paul Sartre says you lack, *you*
repeat *it*. This is not the essential struggle.
You will always be a pastiche of yourself
and an automaton whether you fight it by
affecting desperate changes in tone and
character or chasing moment-to-moment

authenticity. Hypervigilance is an immune
suppressant. You poetry will always be
a pastiche of itself. Or worse, a pastiche of

DAVID
EGGLETON:
     Greta Thunberg is the essential struggle
     self-actualised as a Swedish teenybopper.
     Greta Thunberg striding through
     Typhoon Hagibis like Godzilla crushing fragile
     angry men on the internet in her claws.
     Great Thunberg at the UN thonks down
     a Gandalf staff: you shall not get a PASS.
     Greta Thunberg actual truth to actual power
     speaker. Great Thunberg's power scowl
     zaps grown-ups with its shame ray.
     Greta Thunberg, figurehead on the *Good Ship*
     Lollipop as it hits an iceberg calved
     from the last remnant of the Arctic.

     Greta Thunberg's actual middle name is Tintin.
     Greta Thunberg lifts a pigtail and listens
     to the scientists. Greta Thunberg adds a PS,

     not the three they quote on Breitbart.
     Greta Thunberg plays chess with Death
     in black and white like Max von Sydow.
DEATH
GROANS:
          Don't teensplain carbon to me, Greta
          Thunberg, you try rebelling against extinction
          when you're mortgaged to the eye holes!

Climate deniers don't deny there is a climate,
but if there is one it was made by Hillary Clinton
and Isis. Three monkeys clutch their
sensory apparatus: see no climate crisis.
The essential struggle though is to slither down
off one's high horse, not so much to listen
to the unbearable multitudes thought-shrieking,

but to work on stomaching the worst truth:
the essential struggle is accepting that no one
has to do what you think they should.

They Should've Sent an Influencer

'Today, in the whole history of the world, it's my birthday.'
—London Kills Me (Hanif Kureishi)

Everyone has their time – goes the jingle –
to clonk out into the limelight,
to let that burning lime's candoluminescence throw

their features into relief,
hyperreal, sunlike, and arrayed
with tendril shadows snaking black into the velvet
of the backcloth. Everyone a time,
and for every time a person. This is yours.

Reach. Snatch at it with your elaborations of peace and
kindness, bread and candour.
Bottle it like memory.

Sell it for free to the sick, the half-blind and sand-blind.
Give it a lemon spotlight. Bejazzle it with spaffed glitter
handwriting. As it twists, bespectacle it, add bunny lugs,
balloons, a flash of thunder from forehead to chin like
Jacinda Bowie. No: minimise. Let the brand tell

its story. The morning light the window's hills sing.
Shadows burbling. A child shimmering, who takes
a sashayed step, takes it back, repeats.

It's how one talks business, the talking and not the business.

It's why heads lift, fingers tap, scroll, pinch.
This is their story you are telling of yourself.

At balance teeter anxiety, joy, vanity, yelping, relativism,

tigers, platters, psycho splatters.

All for the drawing in, the seating at your outdoor table,
are these flourishes and motifs, and affirmations

for their loyalty of looking. Preparing them for the real sell.

It is again your birthday. One must be all the ages.
And all the ages you have been are past, and the new
ones are hungry waiting.

This is your moment, your audience landlocked
to their living rooms, or hiding on bath chairs flicking
through your plays on light and motherhood.
This isn't the worst day of your life,
though the restaurants are bolted closed

and I have bought you a present no husband should
ever buy his wife, even if she had asked for it,
but asked for it if he passed a supermarket, not wrapped

to double its unintended but now italic insult,
mouthwash. The streets are barricaded in a war
on the pandemic and it was all I . . . could . . .
But this is your limelit opportunity.
If you don't seize it like a bear salmon,

the first one slopping out of its grip, but then
munch, right in the kisser, you are a debutante,
a wonder of the glare.

Knock Knock. Who's There?
Nietzsche. Nietzsche Who? Nietzsche
to Open ze Door Please a Liddle Bit

I'm not that kind of comedian.
Not funny-haha. More funny-hmm.
Funny-curious.

You won't be gripping your sides, worrying about intestinal prolapse.
Hernia-proof comedy, I am purveying.
Have you heard of alternative comedy?

Have you heard of meta-comedy, or anti-comedy?
Jokes that aren't meant to be funny in themselves,
but funny in their critique of the joke's teller,

funny in their misdirection or their structure?
How many home-DIY bores does it take
to put in a row of recessed downlights?

I am not that kind of comedian.
Nor will I be telling you about my hysterical misfortune.
I won't be saying, buses are weird, aren't they?

I won't start a conversation between two characters,
and move to the left and to the right as I embody them.
I won't say, can I get a WOOT WOOT.

Pratfalls? Physical comedy? No.
And this isn't a persona.
This isn't a humorous persona, such as a Lotto winner who

stays in their admin job at a pest control business
because they have no other friends.
Comedy has no friends.

Comedy is the last line of defence against dogma and puritanism.
The other lines of defence had best be
better suited to the job or we're all fucked.

And we are.
Only comedy can say this with a straight face.
Welcome to the gallows.

Not funny-oh-that's-delicious.
Not funny-thank-you-I-needed-that.
Not funny-funny.

But funny-sorry. Funny-that-can't-be-true-but-I-know-it-is.
Funny-sickened.
Funny-I've-fallen-and-I-can't-get-up.

Funny-the-last-eleven-years-of-Nietzsche's-life-
following-a-paralysing-stroke-and-psychosis.
I'm not that kind of comedian either.

We'll Go from There

(Two eavesdropped phone calls)

He had his money spread around.
We're not talking about millions of dollars.
Thousands. I say we'll get all of it in one.
Probated.
Everyone thinks it's a good idea.

Not the banks. *Not the banks.*
I tell them they're stealing his money.
I give them absolute arseholes.
They keep going on about bank rules,
and I say if it's not the law of the land

it's not *my* rules.
If those people do their jobs
I wouldn't have to be arrogant.
Heh heh. That's right. Okay matey,
I'll catch you later. Bye. Bye.

Hello. How did you do?
Did you enjoy it or . . . different?
Sorry I had to run away but
that man's got dementia.
He's not very well.

And I had to take him away.
I take him along with me.
But when he says I want to go home,
you have to go.
You see all sorts. That guy,

that English guy, he was the top inspector
in the police force in England.
You wouldn't know that, would you.
You keep ahold of that stuff and I'll get a bag
to put it in and we'll go from there.

Mutt Witness

Another negligible mutter I hum,
gum-suck and chew during voiced
pauses – to which another might offer
patience, impatience,

affront, anguish, gestures designed to
inspire expansion of my point to
the realm of human words,
a tut, a cough or a see-sawing

sideways of the head,
with an involuntary yawn sitting
somewhere at a tolerable median –
you draw out. I continue.

(The planets wade in their orbits.)
I touch at my point with a gloved paw, a
gloved jaw. That you bear me sober
teetering over exposition

I appreciate, but resent.
That I have to hear this played over
and over through the weekend
by that reliable inner orchestra of shame

I resent. I want a sign
slung around the neck: Do not encourage.
At least the shame memories
from drunken rantings, or, gag forfend,

dancing, are blunted by alcohol.
In my mumbled opinion I lack only
courage, self-insight and the emotional
intelligence to express myself.

White Pants

I'll have four flat whites, two large, one soy,
one spilt all over the tabletop
and onto my new white pants.
Who wears white pants?
Always they are *new* white pants,
because no detergent
actually removes coffee stains from crotches – nor
the smears on the hips where
one's grubby little fingers
unconsciously wipe themselves.
Who wears them then?
Rich people.
The order is to go. I am too rich
to fritter my time in your natty establishment.
I'm not dashing off to buy NapiSan.
These are going straight in the bin.
I have a closetful of others.

Always Saying Sorry

(an email from Kate)

Well, sorry anyway I was a grump
this morning. All the time in fact. You know
I really love you. You're no rubbish dump.
It's just at home when I am really low
it's suffocating, and I feel like
you make more mess for me to have to clean.
I know I get to hang out with the tyke.
I'm grateful that I can. But does that mean
the rest of my existence has to be
discounted? I'm exhausted all the time,
and tired of never having money. We
are wasting our potential. Still. So I'm
depressed, stuck here while time just disappears.
I realise it's been like this for years.

Email to Cilla

There is a journal, Cilla, proffering
a hundred bucks for poems over lockdown:
Stasis. So I'm trying to write some schlock down.

The snow-bright shaving foam was offering
a backdrop to my teeth this morning. They'd
appeared spectacularly yellow, which
reminded me of Dr Stankiewicz,
a dentist, who, assessing colour, laid
a crown against my fangs and made a tut.
He then proceeded through the spectrum: pale
lemon . . . buttercream . . . straw-blonde. . . sand . . . ale . . .
ginger . . . sick/wan . . . hazel . . . cashew nut . . .
then mustard! . . . ochre! . . . What a humbling onslaught.

So anyway, some piece on this, I thought.

Lockdown

Shall I compare you to a mangled haystack?
Yeah. Well shut thy clang-hole's hoop and scuttle
yonwards like an ocelot. It's payback
that the fossil got the eight-track's rebuttal
not indelibly or pot-and-kettle
black apostle, what. But I'm dissembling.
I will try again to let it settle.
Shall I compare you to what you're resembling?
Shall I compère the ember of the evening's
emblem? When a peregrine or penguin's
denim feather feelings feed where needlings
need the heeding, my comparing strengthens,
their summer hot enough to simmer fish in.
Shall I say, kneel and heal thyself, physician?

Today, I Set about Laying the Macro-Decking Floor of the Den

(after an email from Richard Reeve)

A day or so ago, I rediscovered
this now-mouldy leather satchel. It's
the one in which I used to wedge my bits
of work in progress. I called it a cupboard,
or, more drily, an external colon.
Lost around oh-one, it drifted back
to me again a decade on, the sac
still in a boot: the cops had found the stolen
car, a friend's, who'd parked it near the Crown.
It was a capsule of a prior traitor:
books, a photo, poems that I later
changed. And here again, abloom with down.
Beneath the floor of the den it goes – ambitious
in its mould.
                        As ever, superstitious.

Instead of Finishing 'The Plotz' I've . . .
It's Another . . . Gah!

'The Plotz' I'm writing in ottava rima:
alternating rhymes across a sextain
and then a couplet, this entire schema
in pentameter. Can I, ah, explain
why? I can't. It's tough and I regret it.
But whenever I pick up Don Juan,
Byron's, I remember why it whetted
that ottava rima for a shoo-in.
His poem is just wonderful – with shipwrecks,
cannibals and sex, true love loved blindly,
self-conceit, and wacky rhymes in triplex.
Mine's unfinished. Ashleigh's kindly
left a gap for it in section one.
But really there's no chance I'll get it done.

Noise Control

A capon is, according to the Oxford,
a castrated cock – *a rooster* – fattened
for the eating. Not aware the cocks had
had this done, we ate a couple, that, and
they were quite delectable, our – what
exactly? I suppose – our squeamishness? –
well, probably not mattering a jot.

And on encountering the heinousness
of prog that blasted out the front-room curtain
of the neighbour's cottage down the bank,
the word returned to mind. And I made certain
if not capon cock rock now, a shank
would come. I called the council on the band.
'Yeah no they're not too loud,' I said, *'too bland.'*

No More Experimental Reincarnated Cat Poetry

(For Kate at 36)

I am cat, well,
born again as cat, but was dog, your dog.

But cat before that.

Unless was dog before was cat was dog was cat.
Don't know. Skull hurt. Cat head small.

Still your dog!

Bark meows when you go by.
You see me! Heart go BONK BONK.

Run away though cos am cat.

When was dog I lick paw to show you I cat.
Get gross problem with paw from too much lick.

You love me!

Your husband dumb.
Big dumb dumb.

When you hit him back when dog

I bark dog barks and bite him too to say
stop, no hitting. Peace.

He dumb but no hitting.

Limericks Collaged from the *Withnail & I* Screenplay

Murder and . . . rape and . . . All-Bran . . .
What a piece of work is a man . . .
As a youth I would weep . . .
I know you're not asleep . . .
Get in the back of the van!

. . . me towards the Royal Shakespeare . . .
Grab its ring . . . bag up . . . show no fear . . .
What's you name, McFuck?
Indeed . . . Raymond Duck . . .
Get that damned little swine out of here!

And now I'm calling you one . . .
All right you can stay but the gun . . .
. . . in your toolbox? . . . Liar!
Fucking kettle's on fire!
Something's got to be done.

The Coal Man two weeks ago . . .
. . . busted coming back through Heathrow . . .
I've just spent an hour . . .
All along the watchtower . . .
What . . . ? That's what I want to know.

All Milk under the Exit Ramp

(Seven Poems of Our Seventh Anniversary Weekend)

I'm wet not angry:
I leapt from the shower
to answer your call.

**

Our lives are terrifying. As I clean the toilet
I feel the sick thud of emotion
in the gut. Happy anniversary,

your cat is dead.
Or worse, maybe dead. A neighbour rang us
having broken up a multi-cat fight.

The number was on the collar left at the scene.
No cat, just a lot of silver fur, blood.
We circled the neighbourhood, calling,

your voice plaintive, mine false confident,
and returned home, pushing at despair
like wrists against dough.

**

I'll say mothers not parents.
Mothers chase part-time work.
I'll say mothers not parents.

Employers need full-time workers.
They need them, like fish need
full-time seawater if the form says so.

So the full-time workers sit on
their arses and yak their way through Friday.
Women in their thirties are skilled,

knowledgeable and ambitious,
and mothers may work harder,
I'll say mothers not parents,

but 34 hours is not 37 and a half hours
and the form says 37 and a half hours
and if I was to go back to HR

they wouldn't get back to me.
And what is expertise, knowledge and
ambition? If you already worked here,

you could have those. We are
very flexible. But parents need to know.
I say parents not mothers.

This is what parents sacrificed their
ambition for. I'll say parents, but
under my breath I'll say . . . no

this is in writing. What would HR say?
HR say we'll get back to you.
HR say this is a full-time position.

**

A bottle of milk.
We were leaving the car park.
I'd left it on top.

//

WHACK THUMP – I dash out.
All over the exit ramp,
expressionism.

**

Our lives terrify.
Disasters, gashed hope, sunburn.
But I do love it.

**

Our hearts are like owls.
I hear you call his name out.
The cat slides back in.

// NEAR FUTURE //

Pronouncements of the Visiting Entity, from Behind the Pipe

(written for an animatronic art installation that speaks one of these randomly after a button is pushed)

Can you help me down from here? Not physically. The idea of me. Leave me up here but help the idea of me down.

We have a saying: My tentacle is itchy. You know?

Don't caress the button. Weigh into it. I am speaking on behalf of your saggy tendons.

You are too close to me with no sunblock on. Think it through, warm-blood.

Important: if you hybridise the amphibian and the bacteriophage with yourself, it will only be funny from a long way off . . . I see I am too late.

Our great prophet, call her Juanita the Peripatetic, warned us. We ignored her. She was wrong anyway.

A storm came. I am using metaphor. We have no storms. So I don't know what I mean. But it came.

Have you come to tell my fortune? I know you're right, but I'm sick of that garbage.

Tell your friend Rebecca to come here. I have something to tell her. Or if not her somebody with the same name, or she has something to tell me, or to an entity with the same thoracic webbing.

I can smell the stink of the Manukau Harbour from here.

That warm-blood in the anorak behind you, no back towards the second-hand word shop, he thought I was here to warn you of extinction.

That warm-blood back towards the second-hand word shop is . . . to translate from an ancient sea proverb of my homeworld . . . a real ning-nong.

The bipedal thing is a neat balancing trick. Enough's enough though.

I'm not here to complain about your space junk. But if I were . . . do I talk to you about it?

I see you are a multi-organism creature, warm-blood. Who is in charge there?

Take me to your puppet figurehead mouthpiece. Ha!

Hildegard the Armless once said: Alien technology is only as good as the helpdesk bot.

Do you have any photos of cats?

I'll never get to Te Kūiti. Or some entity will have burned it down before I arrive. I'll think: Who would live in this ash? I would.

Did you take them? Are you trying to oppress me? Or have you seen my leg warmers?

We have infiltrated your governments. Well, not yet, but we're very keen to. Any ideas how to do that?

Weakness is for the kindly. Kindness is for the weakly.

On my homeworld we have love but no music. Love without music is like ethanol without regret. But what would I know.

My favourite word in your warm-blood language is fghjkjhghjk.

The truth is not out there.

Your suffering is all down to the person beside you. Keep a tally of their wrongdoing and announce it to them often. You are innocent.

On my homeworld we have no sarcasm, or only enough to get by.

I was told to watch out for alluring entities who would steal my data while I slept. If only.

My carbon levels are low. Can you burn something please? Something abstract. Down to the ground.

Consciousness is just unconsciousness intercut by occasional jolts where you realise you have forgotten your bag.

A compliment: Your organs look mostly disease free from here.

A compliment: Your fingers look like a hatchling.

Whenever you push that, I worry you are trying to mate with me. I just don't think we have enough in common.

At night I talk to the crustaceans known as woodlice, although they prefer to be called slaters.

Advice from a planet of coal parasites who know: Be persistent when rejected. Wear them down.

My senior podling always said: You can't eat plastic, with the obvious exception of polyvinyl chloride.

I would go to war to get some sleep around here.

You want an aphorism? You can never be too slimy.

I've got beak-ache from the lack of UV, indigestion from the gravity, the smell I won't get into, and that's me sorry making it, but I'm not complaining, am I.

You will meet a tall dark stick of graphite.

Psst. What's the deal with pancakes?

I need to walk back some of these pronouncements a little. I am preposterously drunk on nitrogen.

I don't know what you're smoking, because that's a pitiful little fume trail.

Yellowbeard of the Seam was my public relations consultant, but he-slash-it perished on the trip here. Not an excuse per se. A wondrousness.

It is the greatest freedom to speak one's mind and fear the outcome.

I am from an advanced society of interacting entities where there is no condescension towards little backwards bumpkins like yourselves.

What the drat?

It is the speech-generating device that makes me sound pompous, normally that's undetectable.

On the paradise satellite and casino above the planet Def Skynyrd everything is permitted except exclamation marks.

Oh poor little residents of Karori, frightened of wild pigs!

We all deserve to be imagined despicable.

There's a great acronym we use that I can't remember. No one can, to be honest. And our orthography would mystify you anyway. I'll go behind the pole.

Tell me something and I will pretend to listen while imagining you chewing on a straw.

Humans in two words: lazy arsonists.

Don't push the button yet, wait until a crowd gathers. Every entity's favourite type of waiting.

You would think I could juggle or something. But no, hopeless.

Don't get so angry at idiots. To me you are all irritating bunglers.

In the bureaucracy of the blind, the one-eyed lead advisor has just moved the meeting time so that it clashes with lunch.

We have a saying: You can always lick an ember. It's just exasperating.

Hearing my pronouncements opens a portal in your thinking to my perspective. We call this a rabbit hole, after the graves made by sand rabbits when they are unsuccessful at mating.

If you never forget me I will own a corner of your thinking. Part of you becomes me. Too small to matter, unless you are as gormless as your knuckles suggest.

Hark! In the great cataclysm our homeworld was destroyed by ice. We had found somewhere much better long before, and only the cultists had remained. Oh how, in our fashion, we laughed.

Notes

p.14: The poem 'House, Kid, Dog' appeared in my collection *Back with the Human Condition*. It appears in two versions: pessimistic and less pessimistic. That didn't work for this sequel.

p.24: I was originally Nicholas Croft Brook. The mean boys at school made 'Nick Brook' into a chicken noise. There, that was a lot quicker than the poem.

p.30: This was written for an anthology of children's poetry (*Skinny Dip*), and I am shouting that disclaimer here. Luckily I am not good at writing for children, and it is age-appropriate for you too.

p.44: Jon Cox has become devilishly good at painting. Most in his range would fall under expressionism, so are fun to talk nonsense about. At first I would respond as though I was a phoney baloney art critic, finding meaning where there were just pleasing shapes and colour. Luckily, I regressed to insults. Compiled here and passed off as poetry.

p.54: The brief for this for a Verb Festival gala opening was for the writers involved to speak on 'the essential struggle'. I am not bashing David Eggleton here, whose work I admire. It's the flattery of pastiche.

p.67: I have an obnoxious habit of mincing other people's words into sonnets. The other in this book is from an email of Richard Reeve (p.70). It's a way of practising the art without having to have the ideas. A way of hiding even. On this occasion it was as a response to a particularly devastating email from Kate. I didn't know how to respond and poemifying it somehow seemed to honour the sentiment without having any solution. Kate has given permission to use her words.

p.71: This is about writing the poem 'The Plotz' for my last collection, *Moral Sloth*. In fact I did finish the poem and you should borrow someone's copy of that book and . . . see that I did.

p.72: The brief for this sonnet was to write an accompanying poem to a short film of the same name: watch it online. If you Google 'show me your shorts noise control' the film will come up. An excellent documentary-slash-cartoon.

p.74: I posted this on the Facebook fan page for *Withnail & I*. It received more views and comments than any single other poem I have ever written. Write for the niche nutbars is the lesson learned.

p.81: I'm just going to say it. I'm writing a comedy science fiction novel and this one is the closest in tone to that. Here it appears as a series of one-liners, in poem-like form, but it's also a base script for a tentacled sculpture. The sculpture itself, which I haven't seen at the time this goes to print, will say some of these pronouncements and randomly, and maybe it will make its own variations. You can tweet it at @visiting_entity (not managed by me).

Acknowledgements

Especial thanks first off to my friend and co-parent Kate Wanwimolruk. There are four birthday poems here, and others chart our separation, including one in Kate's own words (ish). Kate, you have been unfailingly supportive of my poems even when they dealt with stuff that was tough for you too. Much thank-youing.

To all the poor shlubs I fire my poems at in a burst of enthusiasm when I've just written them, *cin cin!* James Brown, Ashleigh Young, Blair Reeve, Cilla McQueen, Richard Reeve, Michael Steven, David Kārena Holmes, Rebecca Hawkes, Jim McNaughton, Hamish Ironside and Andy Paterson – thanks and prepare for more.

None of this book was written during my Surrey Hotel–Newsroom writing residency in 2020, but it was supposed to have been, so an apologetic thanks go to the beautiful Surrey Hotel, to Newsroom, and to Steve Braunias.

Thanks to all the people behind the magazines, anthologies, websites, readings and festivals in which and at which many of these poems first appeared: Susan Paris, Kate De Goldi, Claire Mabey, Andrew Laking, Mark Pirie, Emma Neale, Trevor Landers, Paula Green, Jay Nieuwland, Caro DeCarlo, Nikki Lee Birdsey and Rebecca H again. Poems appearing elsewhere first are as follows: 'Great-Grandad Rants over Current Affairs' (*Skinny Dip*, 2021); 'House, Kid, ~~Dog~~ Divorce' and 'You Will Find Me Much Changed' (performed as part of the Loemis event Epilogue, with the latter appearing in *Sweet Mammalian*); 'Instead of Finishing "The Plotz" I've . . . It's Another . . . Gah!', 'No More Experimental Reincarnated Cat Poetry' and 'We'll Go from There' (*Broadsheet*); 'Knock Knock. Who's There? Nietzsche. Nietzsche Who? Nietzsche to Open ze Door Please a Liddle Bit' (*Landfall*); 'Noise Control' (*Singlets, Shorts and Briefs, Poems from the 2020 NZ Show Me Your Shorts! Film Festival 2020*, 2021); 'Poem for Derek' (*Glottis Zero*); 'Pronouncements of the Visiting Entity, from Behind the Pipe' (written for a talking artwork in Loemis 2022) 'They Should've Sent an Influencer' (Poetry Shelf); 'They're Playing the "You've Gone on Too Long" Music, but the Essential Struggle Is to Think Yourself More Important Than the Schedules of Plebeians' (written for Verb Festival 2019, appearing first in Food Court zine, *Another One*).

Thanks as ever to the . . . I want to say 'sterling', but what does that mean really? Shiny? Metallic? . . . to the . . . shimmering and luminous staff at THWUP. Fergus, Ashleigh, Craig, Tayi, and especially whoever else you've roped in. You are too kind.

Thanks to Kushana Bush for the cover art. You are hilarious.